Life in a
DESERT CACTUS

Jill Bailey

Chicago, Illinois

Copyright © 2004 Raintree
Published by Raintree, a division of Reed Elsevier, Inc.
Chicago, Illinois
Customer Service 888-363-4266
Visit our website at www.raintreelibrary.com

All rights reserved. No part of this publication may be reproduced or utilized in any form or by any means, electronic or mechanical, including photocopying, recording, or by any information storage and retrieval system, without permission in writing from the publishers.

For information, address the publisher:
Raintree, 100 N. LaSalle, Suite 1200, Chicago, IL 60602

Project Editors: Geoff Barker, Marta Segal Block, Jennifer Mattson, and Tamsin Osler
Production Director: Brian Suderski
Illustrated by Stuart Lafford
Consultant: Michael Chinery
Designed by Rob Norridge and Ian Winton
Picture Research by Rachel Tisdale

Planned and produced by Discovery Books

Library of Congress Cataloging-in-Publication Data:
Bailey, Jill.
Life in a desert cactus / Jill Bailey.
v. cm. -- (Microhabitats)
Includes bibliographical references and index.
Contents: Desert cacti -- Cactus diner -- The hunters move in -- Desert shelter.
ISBN 0-7398-6801-2 (lib. bdg.-hardcover) -- ISBN 1-4109-0347-8 (pbk.)
1. Saguaro--Juvenile literature. 2. Saguaro--Ecology--Sonoran Desert--Juvenile literature.
3. Desert ecology--Sonoran Desert--Juvenile literature. [1. Saguaro. 2. Cactus. 3. Desert animals. 4. Desert ecology. 5. Ecology.]
I. Title. II. Series.
QK495.C11B313 2003
583'.56--dc21
2003002657

Printed and bound in the United States.
08 07 06 05 04
10 9 8 7 6 5 4 3 2 1

Acknowledgments
The publishers would like to thank the following for permission to reproduce photographs:
Cover and p.12 top: Dan Griggs/Natural History Photographic Agency; p.6: Hans Reinhard/Oxford Scientific Films; p.7: Joe McDonald/Bruce Coleman Collection; p.9: Jeff Foott/Bruce Coleman Collection; p.10: Wendy Shattil & Bob Rozinski/Oxford Scientific Films; p.11: Paul Berquist/AA/Oxford Scientific Films; p.12 bottom: Photo Disc; p.13: Lon E. Lauber/Oxford Scientific Films; p.14: Zig Leszczynski/AA/Oxford Scientific Films; p.15: Claude Steelman/SAL/Oxford Scientific Films; p.16: Joe McDonald/AA/Oxford Scientific Films; p.17 top: Jeff Foott/Bruce Coleman Collection; p.17 bottom: Jeff Foott/Bruce Coleman Collection; p.18: Owen Newman/Oxford Scientific Films; p.19: Daniel Heuclin/Natural History Photographic Agency; p.20 top: J. Highet/Art Directors & Trip Photo Library; p.20 bottom: Harold Taylor/Oxford Scientific Films; p.21: David Middleton/Natural History Photographic Agency; p.22: John Cancalosi/Bruce Coleman Collection; p.24: John Shaw/Natural History Photographic Agency; p.25: M.P.L. Fogden/Bruce Coleman Collection; p.26: Corbis; p.27: Zig Leszczynski/Oxford Scientific Films; p.28: Stan Osolinski/Oxford Scientific Films; p.29: Granville Harris/Bruce Coleman Collection.

Some words are shown in bold, **like this.** You can find out what they mean by looking in the glossary.

Contents

Desert Cacti	4
Cactus Diner	10
The Hunters Move In	16
Desert Shelter	22
The Desert Landscape	28
Glossary	30
Further Reading	31
Index	32

Desert Cacti

A cactus is a swollen, fleshy plant with lots of spines. A cactus is a **succulent**, which means it is full of stored water. What makes a cactus different from all other plants are the cushionlike structures, called **areoles**, found all over its surface. The areoles have clusters of spines and, at certain times of year, flowers. Most cacti (more than one cactus are called cacti) are leafless. There are many shapes and sizes of cactus, ranging from buttonlike peyotes only a few inches high to giant **saguaros** over 75 ft (23 m) tall.

This illustration shows some of the many animals that live and feed on and around desert cacti.

Cactus Giant

Most cacti are found in the deserts of North and South America. A few grow in wetter places and some live in high mountains. This book is mostly about the saguaro. Thousands of saguaro grow in the Sonoran Desert, which is in the south-western United States and Mexico. Saguaro National Park, in southern Arizona, is a landscape of mountains and desert, where temperatures often exceed 100 °F (over 37 °C).

Guess What?

There are over 1,600 different species, or kinds, of cacti.

Cacti have been around for about 30–40 million years.

A fully grown saguaro can weigh about 4,000 lb (over 1,800 kg)—as much as five medium-sized cars.

Surviving in the Desert

A plant uses its leaves to make food, taking energy from sunlight, **nutrients** and water from the soil, and carbon dioxide gas from the air. Tiny holes in the leaf surface, called **stomata**, allow gases in and out of the leaf, but water can also escape from them. Most leaves have a large surface area, so they lose water easily.

The cardon cactus from Baja, California is the largest cactus in the world. It may live for 300 years, reaching a height of 70 feet (21 meters) and a weight of 23 tons. These cacti are well spaced out because their roots compete for water.

A desert gets very little rain and the strong sun makes water **evaporate** quickly from a plant's surface. Desert cacti save water by having no leaves. Instead, they make their food in their fat, green stems. **Succulent** stems have a small surface area compared to their volume, so they lose less water. The stem is covered in a thick, waxy coat to reduce water loss.

Expanding Cacti

Most cactus stems have a series of vertical **furrows**, or ridges and folds, like an accordion. The little stomata are deep in the furrows, protected from the wind, so they do not lose much water. When the cactus soaks up rain with its roots, it swells up and the "accordion" expands. As the water evaporates, the cactus shrinks back and the furrows become deeper again. Because it does not rain very often in the desert, the cactus needs to soak up as much water as possible when it does rain. Many cacti have long roots close to the soil surface to catch the rain before it evaporates.

The cactus stem has a series of ridges and folds. Each ridge has a row of starry clusters of spines.

See for Yourself

To see how its waxy coat stops a cactus stem from drying out, you will need two sponges, two plastic containers, some wax paper, and water. Soak the sponges in the containers of water, and cover one of them with wax paper. Leave both of them to dry. See which sponge dries out first.

Growth of a Giant

When a **saguaro** seed **germinates**, or begins to grow, the little seedling needs shade and shelter. For the first few years it grows under the shade of a tree, such as the palo verde.

As it grows, the saguaro changes from a small, round shape, to a slimmer, more pillar-like shape. By the time it is 80 years old the mature saguaro will have several arms.

The young saguaro grows very slowly—less than 6 inches (16 centimeters) in height in its first 10 years. After 25 years, it is two feet (60 centimeters) tall. As it grows taller, it becomes slimmer too. By the time it is 50 years old, it will be as tall as a palo verde—about 10 feet (3 meters). At about 60 years old, the saguaro starts to grow arms.

Bursting into Flower

By this time, the saguaro cactus is developed enough to produce flowers. From now on it will flower every spring. The flowers appear at the tip of the cactus. They are white with bright yellow centers. By midsummer, the flowers ripen into fruits which have red flesh packed with little black seeds.

Many old saguaros have several arms and look a little like branching candlesticks. A saguaro will go on growing slowly until it is about 200 years old.

Each saguaro flower opens in late afternoon for just one day.

See for Yourself

Buy two cacti of the same kind and size from a garden or flower store. Measure around the middle of each cactus, and note the size of each one. Beware of the spines and remember to wear thick gloves. Water one regularly for several weeks, but keep the other dry. Measure the two cacti again and compare the results with their earlier sizes. The cactus with no water should have shrunk. Water it and see how soon it expands again.

Cactus Diner

A Feast of Flowers

Cactus flowers produce a yellow powder called **pollen**. At the base of the flower petals is a sweet-smelling, sugary liquid called **nectar**. The pollen and nectar attract insects and other animals, which become dusted with pollen as they feed. If the pollen is rubbed off on another plant of the same kind, that flower may become fertilized. The flower needs this to happen in order to produce seeds—it is called **pollination**.

A hummingbird's long bill and tongue allow it to sip nectar deep in the flowers.

Tiny cactus bees feed on the nectar and carry pollen back to feed their young. Bees have long tube-like tongues that suck up the nectar. Butterflies' tongues are so long that they keep them curled up like a spring when not in use. At night moths and bats come to feed from the flowers.

The jackrabbit's huge ears have a lot of small blood vessels close to the surface of the skin. This allows heat from the blood to pass into the air, cooling the animal.

A Prickly Feast

Although the cactus has spines, some animals actually eat the **saguaro**, especially when it is young and its skin is not tough. The water stored in its flesh is a welcome treat in the desert. Desert rats eat tender cactus seedlings. Jackrabbits often nibble at a fleshy cactus while they enjoy the shade it provides.

Guess What?

When the saguaro is in flower, there are many cactus bees' nests in the ground around the cactus. An area the size of 2–3 tennis courts may contain hundreds of thousands of nests.

While it hovers, a hummingbird's wings beat up to 80 times a second. Its heart beats 1,260 times a minute.

Feeding the Birds

Flocks of birds wander around the desert looking for food. They can spot the bright red fruits of the **saguaro** from far away. The thrasher feeds on cactus fruits in winter. Like the woodpecker, the thrasher has a narrow, pointed beak that allows it to catch insects among the cactus spines. White-winged doves and groups of quails feed on the ground, where they scratch around for cactus seeds.

The thrasher has a sharp beak for catching insects.

The Gambel's quail feeds mainly on plants. It lives on the ground, and rests in the shade of saguaros and other cacti in the middle of the day.

A Banquet on the Ground

Peccaries—which look like small wild pigs—and ground squirrels wander from one cactus to another in search of juicy cactus fruits. They hunt in small, family groups. Their good sense of smell helps them to find food.

Mice scuttle all over cacti, eating anything they can find. Lizards such as the large, fat chuckwalla will climb cacti in search of flowers and fruits, which they like to eat. They also search on the ground for fallen fruits. Chuckwalla lizards like to sunbathe in the early morning before they set out to search for food.

Peccaries feed on cactus fruits, insects, and small reptiles. They also dig for roots and worms.

Guess What?

When danger looms, the chuckwalla lizard hides in a crevice and puffs up its body with air to jam itself into the crack. This makes it difficult for its enemies to pull it out.

Ground squirrels raise their large, bushy tails and hold them over their heads like parasols to shade them from the sun.

The Hoarding Habit

Many desert animals store seeds in their **burrows** between the roots of the **saguaro** in case food becomes scarce later in the year. Kangaroo rats and pocket mice stuff saguaro seeds into pouches in their cheeks and carry them back to their burrows. They seldom drink but get their water from the **succulent** plants they eat.

The Gila monster can live for months on fat stored in its tail.

Packrats (also known as woodrats), pocket gophers, and harvester ants also hoard seeds underground. Leafcutter ants carry pieces of leaf and stem to their homes and grow special **fungi** on them, which the ants like to eat. The Gila monster, a poisonous lizard, stores body fat in its thick tail. In times of **drought** it can change some of this fat into water.

Rats' Nests

Packrats build their nests in branching cacti, whose spines protect the rats from **predators**. Only the badger, Gila monster, and snakes can get in to eat the rat and its young. Their nests are made up of a messy pile of twigs, sticks, branches, and cactus spines. They keep out the heat of the sun during the day, and protect the rat from the cold of the desert night.

Guess What?

Packrats pass their nests from one generation to the next. Some packrat nests are nearly 40,000 years old.

Over many centuries packrat nests collect traces of the plants and animals that lived in there. These remains are very valuable because scientists can learn a lot about the past by studying them.

Packrat nests make a good home for rattlesnakes during the winter. The rat seals the snakes into a chamber in the burrow with a wall of twigs. Snakes are very slow and lazy when cold, so they are no threat to the rats then.

Packrats love to decorate their nests with bright, shiny objects such as coins, keys, and jewelry.

The Hunters Move In

The Day Shift

The small animals that come to feed around cacti attract larger hunters, or **predators**. Small cactus wrens, woodpeckers, and thrashers all like to eat insects. Spiders, too, lie in wait, hidden in the **furrows** of the cactus. They spin webs across the folds, or ribs, of the cactus to trap insects.

Spines pose no problems for the cactus wren, which hunts for insects among the cacti.

Lizards pick their way carefully between the cactus spines as they hunt for flies, beetles, and anything small that moves. Hawks hover in the sky above, their sharp eyes scanning the ground for mice. Ravens look out for dead animal remains on the ground, but they may also attack a desert tortoise.

High-Speed Hunters

Roadrunners can run better than they can fly. They chase after lizards, snakes, and mice. A roadrunner can run as fast as 17 miles per hour (27 kilometers per hour), and can even leap into the air to catch a hummingbird in flight.

The roadrunner can run fast enough to catch lizards.

Larger predators such as the coyote and desert fox search for mice, cottontail rabbits, and quails feeding on the cacti or sheltering among them. These hunters have good hearing, and listen for mice in the undergrowth before pouncing on them. Coyotes live in pairs or small packs, and defend an average hunting **territory** of about ten square miles (26 square kilometers).

The coyote will eat whatever it can find in the desert, from rabbits and ground squirrels to lizards, fruits, and berries.

The Night Shift

Other **predators** are on the prowl around the **saguaro** and other cacti at night. Owls have big eyes and excellent night vision. Their wings have special, very soft feathers, so they make no noise as they fly, and their **prey** have no warning of their approach. Owls seize mice and other animals with their feet, which have powerful, curving claws.

This elf owl has made its home in a saguaro. Despite its tiny size, it can catch and eat scorpions.

The little elf owl, at just six inches (15 centimeters) long from head to tail, is the smallest owl in the world. The pygmy owl is not much bigger. The great horned owl is over three times larger. It hunts over a wide area, looking for fish, lizards, and jackrabbits as well as large insects. It makes different calls, including barks, growls, and screams, and can sound very spooky when it shrieks at night.

Hunting in the Dark

Many snakes, such as rattlesnakes and kingsnakes, hunt at night. Between each eye and nostril, the rattlesnake has a little pit that is sensitive to heat. Rattlesnakes detect mice and other prey by the heat that their bodies give off.

Bats fly around the saguaro hunting moths and other night-flying insects. Spiders and scorpions also leave their homes in or near the cactus to hunt at night. Scorpions seize their prey with their large pincers, but may use the stinger in their tail to **paralyze** it if it struggles.

A Sonoran mountain kingsnake devours a collared lizard. The snake can unhinge its jaw. Its mouth and neck have skin that stretches to allow it to eat large prey.

Guess What?

Tiny hairs on the legs of scorpions can detect the vibrations made by prey on the ground up to one foot (one-third of a meter) away.

Although a scorpion has a powerful stinger in its tail and strong pincers, it may be eaten by a lizard, spider, owl, bat, shrew, or even a centipede.

The kingsnake hunts rattlesnakes. It is not affected by the rattlesnake's poison, and coils round its victim to choke it to death.

Cactus Collectors

Cactus fruits are almost the only sweet food in the desert. For thousands of years local people have used them in syrups, sauces and soups, jam, oils, bread, and candy. They brew **saguaro** wine and in the past held wine feasts that lasted for weeks.

The "pads" of the prickly pear cactus, on sale here in a Mexican market, can be eaten as vegetables. Prickly pear fruits (below) are sweet and juicy.

Native desert peoples used the saguaro in many other ways, too. Its flesh was put on wounds to reduce pain. The seeds were fed to chickens or used in the making of leather from animal skins. Dried ribs of dead saguaros were used to make fences, walls, cradles, shelves, bird cages, baskets, or oars.

Cacti of all shapes and sizes are popular houseplants. They grow best on sunny windowsills.

Cactus Rustlers

Because cacti take so long to grow, and large ones are expensive to buy, some people go into the desert to steal them. People who steal cacti are called cactus rustlers. It is almost impossible to dig up large cacti successfully because of their very delicate, shallow roots, so most stolen cacti do not survive for long.

Sometimes people use saguaros and other cacti for shooting practice. This usually kills the cactus, because it allows water to escape and lets in insects and **fungi**. In some states cacti are protected by law.

Guess What?

The Seri Indians used to paint saguaro fruit juice on their cheeks and noses to bring them good luck.

In 1982 a man from Phoenix was killed when a large saguaro he had shot fell on him.

Desert Shelter

Apartment Buildings

An old **saguaro** may have lots of nest holes at different levels, almost like an apartment building. The little elf owl and the pygmy owl, the Gila woodpecker, and the gilded flicker (another kind of woodpecker) all make their nests there. The woodpeckers peck holes in the cactus stem, and the cactus seals the wound with a hard, corky layer so it does not dry out. This also keeps the nest hole dry. Old woodpecker nests are often used by owls, other birds, like flycatchers and kestrels, rats, and mice.

Harris hawks build messy nests of sticks high up in large saguaros. Here their young are safe from enemies like foxes and coyotes.

White-winged doves feed on cactus fruits, carrying them away and dropping seeds as they feed. This helps the saguaro to spread across the desert. Birds called purple martins also nest in saguaros. High in a spiny cactus, newborn birds are safe from **predators**.

Desert Boots

Old cacti often die when they are brought crashing down by strong winds during a big thunderstorm. Even after dying they are home to many animals. Old nest holes, with their corky lining, form structures called **boots,** which make ideal shelters for mice and snakes. Lizards, scorpions, spiders, millipedes, and thousands of ants and termites soon move into the rotting cactus.

Guess What?

Unlike most other hawks, Harris hawks live in small groups. They may hunt together and even share the care of their young.

A pair of elf owls will sing a duet of whines, barks, and yips. They sound like a couple of young puppies.

The black widow spider often lives in cacti. Its venom is 15 times more deadly than a rattlesnake's.

A broken-off stump of a dead saguaro attracts many different insects, including carpenter ants (left), termites, and scorpions. Old nest holes make a good shelter for pocket mice.

Hidden Homes

Many desert animals live underground. Mice, rats, badgers, ground squirrels, cottontails, Gila monsters, jackrabbits, and foxes live in **burrows** among the roots of the saguaro. Smaller animals like ants and spiders live there, too. Snakes often use old burrows that have been abandoned by other animals.

A gray fox takes shelter from the heat of the desert sun.

Bark beetles chew long tunnels under the bases of nest holes in the **saguaro**. Termites live near the bottom of the cactus. They make their homes from a mixture of soil and saliva. They feed on the dead pieces of cactus that fall to the ground.

The Shy and the Brave

The kangaroo rat has very long, strong hind legs. It never drinks because it gets all the water it needs from its food. This rat hates to be out in the open, and hops rapidly across the desert from one clump of cacti to another, searching for seeds.

Guess What?

- The kangaroo rat keeps itself clean by rolling in dust instead of bathing in water.
- Grasshopper mice communicate with each other using high-pitched squeaks that humans cannot hear.
- The Gila monster's teeth have two grooves in them. When it bites its victim, poison flows down the channels into its prey.

The grasshopper mouse is a fierce **predator**. It kills other mice by biting the backs of their necks, and tackles a scorpion by biting off its stinger before eating it.

A grasshopper mouse howls like a high-pitched wolf to communicate with other members of its family group.

Weathering the Desert

Inside their **burrows,** animals avoid the heat of the day and the cold of night. Tiny droplets of water in their breath make the air in the burrow moist. Some rats and mice seal the entrances to their burrows to keep the moisture in.

A group of burrowing owls keeps watch by the entrance to their underground home.

In the deserts of California and Arizona, the main time for rain is July and August. There are only a few showers and storms during the rest of the year. In winter it can be very cold, with frosts and even snow. Some animals, including snakes, cannot produce their own body heat, but rely on the warmth of their surroundings. In winter they become too slow to hunt, so they sleep in their underground burrows instead. This is called **hibernation**.

Secret Sleepers

Some animals, like pocket mice, find it hard to find food during the dry season, and sleep in cool, underground burrows instead. This dry season sleep is called **estivation**. While they hibernate or estivate, animals use little energy, so they do not burn up much food. Their hearts beat slower and their breathing becomes shallow.

The gopher tortoise spends 95 percent of its time in its burrow, and sleeps through much of the hottest and coldest weather. Several tortoises may share a burrow, each in its own den. Up to 40 different kinds of animals share these burrows, including snakes, mice and rats, burrowing owls, and gray foxes.

The gopher tortoise uses its flattened front legs to dig itself a huge burrow.

Guess What?

- Never pick up a dead rattlesnake. First, it may not be dead! Second, even if it is dead, a powerful nerve reflex may still make it bite and inject poison.

- A rattlesnake's rattle is made of the same material as your fingernails.

- The gopher tortoise can store water in its bladder and absorb it again when it needs it. It can survive a whole year without drinking any water.

The Desert Landscape

Cacti Large and Small

There are many different kinds of desert cacti. They may produce bright white, red, yellow, or orange flowers. Many cactus names are clues to their shape, such as organpipe cactus, hedgehog cactus, fishhook cactus (with hooked spines), ball cactus, melon cactus, living-rock cactus. The old woman cactus and old man cactus have pale woolly hairs.

Chollas are among the spiniest of cacti. Packrats collect pieces of cholla and use them to protect their nests.

Prickly pear cacti look like many small, spiny plates joined together. Sometimes people grow them close together in a row to make a hedge for keeping cattle or people off their property. Their fruits attract birds, peccaries, and many other desert animals.

Cactus Followers

Cacti are very important to the wildlife of the desert. In this dry land, **succulent** cacti often provide desert animals with the only source of water as well as shelter from the blazing sun. The cacti need the animals, too. They **pollinate** the cactus flowers and eat their fruits. The seeds pass out in the animals' droppings and are carried to other places where they may seed and grow into new generations of desert cacti.

The Sonoran Desert is home to many different cacti, including the barrel cactus, the prickly pear with its red fruits, the branching cholla, and giant saguaros.

Glossary

areole small "cushion" bearing clusters of spines and, in some cases, flowers. Cacti are the only plants that have areoles.
boot hollow, corklike remains of cactus burrows that are left after the rest of the cactus has decayed
burrow (verb and noun) to dig a hole or tunnel in the ground. A hole or tunnel used as an animal's home is called a burrow.
drought long, dry period when little or no rain falls
estivation special kind of deep sleep or period of inactivity that helps an animal survive a hot, dry season when food and water are scarce
evaporate change in form from liquid to gas
fungus (plural—fungi) simple organism whose body is made from many tiny threads that spread over whatever it is eating. The threads turn its food into liquid, then absorb it.
furrow groove or deep fold
germinate to sprout. A seed or spore germinates when the new plant or fungus inside it starts to grow.
hibernation special kind of deep sleep during the winter that helps an animal survive a time when food is scarce
nectar sweet-smelling, sugary liquid produced by flowers to attract insects
nutrient anything contained in a food that helps keep a living thing healthy and active, such as minerals, vitamins, and protein
paralyze cause an animal to be unable to move
pollen powdery grains made by flowers to fertilize other flowers of the same kind
pollination transfer of pollen from one flower to another so that the flower can be fertilized and can reproduce

predator animal that hunts another animal for food

prey animal that is hunted by another animal for food

sacred considered very holy

saguaro giant cactus that grows only in western North America. Some can live to be 200 years old.

species group of animals that share certain features and can breed together

stomata tiny holes (too small to see) that allow oxygen to move into a leaf or stem, and water vapor and waste gases to move out of the leaf

succulent (noun and adjective) plant that stores a great deal of water in its stem and leaves (if it has them)

territory area defended by an animal that wants to use it as a shelter, a home to raise its young, or as a place to find food or look for mates

Further Reading

Bash, Barbara. *Desert Giant: The Life of a Saguaro Cactus*. Layton, Utah: Gibbs Smith, 2002.

Giesecke, Ernestine. *Desert Plants*. Chicago: Heinemann, 1999.

Green, Jennifer. *A Saguaro Cactus*. New York: Crabtree, 1999.

Johnson, Rebecca, Gary Braasch and Phyllis Saroof. *A Walk in the Desert*. Minneapolis: Carolrhoda Books, 2001.

Pipes, Rose. *Hot Deserts*. Chicago: Raintree, 1998.

Royston, Angela. *Extreme Survival: Deserts*. Chicago: Raintree, 2004.

Wright-Frierson, Virginia. *A Desert Scrapbook: Dawn to Dusk in the Sonoran Desert*. New York: Aladdin, 2002.

Index

ants 14, 23–24
areoles 4
Arizona 5, 26

badgers 15, 24
bark beetles 24
barrel cactus 4, 29
bats 10, 19
beetles 16
birds 10–12, 16, 22
burrows 14–15, 24, 26-27
butterflies 10

cactus bees 10–11
cactus boots 23
cactus rustlers 21
cactus stem 67, 22
cactus wrens 16
cacti, uses of 20–21, 28
    different kinds of 28
California 26
cardon cactus 6
chollas 9, 29
chuckwallas 13
cottontails 5, 17, 24
coyotes 17, 22

desert peoples 20–21
desert tortoises 16
droughts 14

elf owls 18, 22-23
estivation 27
evaporation 6-7

flies 16
flowers 4, 9-11, 13, 28-29
flycatchers 22
foxes 17, 22, 24, 27
fruits 9, 12-13, 20, 22, 29
fungi 14, 21
furrows 7, 16

germination 8

Gila monster 14-15, 24–25
grasshopper mouse 25
great horned owl 18
ground squirrels 13, 17, 24

harvester ants 14
hawks 4, 16, 22–23
hibernation 26–27
Hispanic peoples 20
hummingbirds 14, 10–11

insects 10, 12–13, 16, 18–19, 21, 23

jackrabbits 10–12, 18, 24

kangaroo rat 25
kestrels 22

leafcutter ants 14
lizards 13, 16–17, 19, 23

Mexico 5, 20
mice 13 16–19, 22–27
millipedes 23
moths 10, 19

nectar 10
nest holes 22–24
North America 5

organpipe cactus 4, 28
owls 18–19, 22, 26–27

packrats 14–15, 28
palo verde 8
peccaries 13
peyotes 4
pocket gophers 14
pocket mice 4, 27
pollen 10
pollination 10, 29
predators 15–18, 22
prickly pears 5, 20, 28–29

purple martins 22

quails 4, 12, 17

rainfall 6-7, 26
rats 11, 22, 24–28
rattlesnakes 5, 15, 17, 19, 27
ravens 16
roadrunners 17
roots 6-7, 13-14, 21, 24

Saguaro National Park 5
saguaros 4–5, 8–9, 11-12, 14, 18, 22, 29
    growth 8
    flesh 11
scorpions 18–19, 23, 25
seedlings 11
seeds 9, 12, 22
Seri Indians 21
snakes 15, 17, 19, 23–24, 26, 27
Sonoran Desert 5, 29
South America 5
spiders 16, 19, 23–24
spines 4, 7, 11–12, 15–16, 28
spring 9
stomata 6
succulents 4, 6, 14, 29
summer 9
sunlight 6, 15, 29

termites 23–24
thrashers 12, 16

water 7, 29
white-winged doves 12, 22
wind 7, 23
winter 12, 15, 26
woodpeckers 12, 16, 22
woodrats (see packrats)
worms 13

Edison Twp. Pub. Library
340 Plainfield Ave.
Edison, NJ 08817
DEC 10 2003